Patterns for Living

Spiritual Growth for Christian Women

IRENE YOUNG MATTOX

Patterns for Living

Spiritual Growth for Christian Women

By
IRENE YOUNG MATTOX

21st Century Christian
2809 Granny White Pike
Nashville, TN 37204

The lessons in this series were taught by Irene Mattox Young during her more than 60 years of Bible study and teaching. They represent the thoughts of a godly woman whose life's influence and teaching have helped countless thousands of Christian women. May they enrich your life to God's glory.

As these lessons were written for oral presentation, it is possible that proper acknowledgment of sources has not been made in every case. We wish to thank any whose contributions may not have been acknowledged.

—M. Norvel and Helen M. Young
  Billie Wesley Silvey
  Editors

About the Author

Irene Young Mattox was born in Seymour, Texas, December 31, 1881. She was the oldest of 13 children of F. L. Young, pioneer preacher and school teacher. She began teaching school in Greenville, Texas, at the age of 17, and at the age of 22, was married to Judge Perry Mattox.

The Mattoxes lived in Grand Falls and Bishop, Texas, and in Bristow and Oklahoma City, Oklahoma. Churches were begun in their home in each of these cities, and these churches continue to serve the cause of Christ.

Mrs. Mattox was invited by the late A. R. Holton to address a group of women in Norman, Oklahoma, in 1927 on " A Christian Woman's Responsibility." She thus became the first woman to address women's groups at lectureships and other religious gatherings among churches of Christ.

She was principal of the Longfellow and Rockwood schools in Oklahoma City in the 1920's, and later organized and headed the Oklahoma County welfare department.

She was founder and state president of Oklahoma's Parent Teacher Association and was the state's official representative when the National Congress paid tribute to PTA pioneers in the early 1950's. She was the organizer, life director and president of Oklahoma City's Big Sisters, a group which continues to help girls in trouble. A member of the Daughters of the American Revolution, former president of the Federated Bible Club and member of the Women's Christian Temperance Union, she also worked for candidates in state and county elections. She felt a keen sense of responsibility to use her every talent, always giving her best of time and energy to her family and the local church.

Mrs. Mattox was a dauntless supporter of Christian education and was instrumental in the formation of three women's organizations to promote Christian colleges—the Stepping Stones of Oklahoma Christian College, Associated Women for Pepperdine University and Lubbock Christian College Associates. In 1963 at a testimonial dinner, she was presented a plaque for her work for Christian colleges by Dr. James O. Baird, president of Oklahoma Christian College. In 1967, the Stepping Stones dedicated their cookbook to her. She received the annual Christian Services Award from Pepperdine in 1968 and the "Woman of the Year" award from 20th Century Christian in 1969.

One of the Mattox's seven children, Dr. F. W. Mattox, served as president of Lubbock Christian College. A son-in-law, Dr. M. Norvel Young, former minister of the Broadway Church of Christ in Lubbock has served as President and Chancellor of Pepperdine University. Her daughter Helen, wife of Dr. M. Norvel Young, follows in her mother's footsteps as a lecturer, author and leader among Christian women.

Mrs. Mattox taught ladies' Bible classes and participated in lectureships and training schools across the nation.

She always was a woman of great courage and deep joy whose radiant faith was contagious. She loved God and his Word supremely. She knew the meaning of grace and the strength which comes from dependence on an all loving, all powerful Savior. Thousands could say, "She has been a good friend to many people and also to me" (Romans 16:2).

Introduction

The Bible class period is an important time for us. What we study, think and learn may change our lives. Shall we take these times and dedicate them to reading, meditation and worship together? God is real! He is aware of each of us! He is able and willing to help us all with our lives!

Are you able to understand your problems? Do you know God? Do you know yourself? Let's make these study periods a sort of retreat, a certain time each week dedicated to "My God and I." Is there anything more important?

Let's not make these meetings just periods of study from God's Word about God; rather, let us bring ourselves to him, to meet and know him. We give much time and study to trying to learn about him. May we go beyond information and knowledge and truly meet him. He will be here! He wants your interest and your love. Rearrange your plans and duties. Give him first place in your life, and he will bless you.

"And this is eternal life: for men to know you, the only true God, and to know Jesus Christ, whom you sent" (John 17:3).

—Irene Y. Mattox

Contents

Lesson I

Look at Yourself

Scriptures for study:
2 Corinthians 13:5
Galatians 5:19, 22-26
Ephesians 5:1-2, 15, 19-21
Philippians 4:4-9
Colossians 3:12-17

The Attraction of Mirrors

"Mirror, mirror on the wall, who's the fairest of them all?" So spoke the evil queen in "Snow White." Mirrors have a magnetic attraction about them. It is difficult to pass one without looking into it. Little girls love to look at themselves in mirrors. In Greek mythology Narcissus wasted away from constantly looking at his reflection in a clear pool.

Have you ever sat in a car parked by the curb and watched people looking at themselves in showroom windows? They adjust their clothes, hold their heads higher, and then go on their way and forget how they look. This is like the man James talks about who "looks in a mirror and sees himself as he is. He takes a look at himself and then goes away, and at once forgets what he looks like." This is the man who hears God's Word but does not apply what he hears. "But the man who looks closely into the perfect law that sets men free, who keeps on paying attention to it, and does not simply listen and then forget it, but puts it into practice—that man will be blessed by God in what he does" (James 1:23-25). Do you read God's Word to change you or as a ritual to make you feel you are a "good Christian"?

Reflecting Christ

As the moon, which has no light of its own, reflects the sun, so followers of Christ will reflect his light. Paul in Ephesians tells us, "Since you are God's dear children, you must try to be like him. Your life must be controlled by love, just as Christ loved us and gave his life for us..." (Ephesians 5:1-2). This is our goal—reflecting Christ. However, all too often we are like the man who sees and then forgets. We look but do not see. We see but do not understand. We understand but through ignorance or lack of interest are inactive. Often our own personalities and problems get in the way of our effectiveness as Christians.

Who Are You, Anyway?

Dr. Norman Vincent Peale tells of a man who received a promotion in his work. He and his wife planned a big celebration dinner to share the good news with their friends. The wife, radiant with pride and joy, went to the supermarket to buy food for the dinner, but while she was

14

shopping, she overheard two ladies standing nearby. "Just who does she think she is, anyway?" one was asking the other. Later, as she started home, the words came back to mind and she glanced at her reflection in the rear view mirror and asked herself, "Who are you, anyway?"

Let us all look at ourselves in the mirror each day and ask the same question. It is essential that we know ourselves. Unless we have some sense of our own good qualities, we cannot use them effectively in God's service. Also, it is necessary that we recognize our weaknesses and faults. "Keep an eye on yourself so that you will not be tempted" (Galatians 6:1).

The National Association of Mental Health gives three questions which indicate whether one is mentally healthy. These also have application to one's spiritual health. Look at yourself in light of these questions and see if you are your most effective self.

1. How do you feel about yourself? Do fears, worry or guilt hamper your effectiveness as a Christian?
2. How do you feel about others? Do you follow Christ's example of love and sympathy to all?
3. How do you meet problems? Do you meet them with the strength available to Christians?

How Do You Feel About Yourself?

In a survey of 50 women from all walks of life, 37 were found to be obsessed with fears—fears for their husbands' jobs and their love, fears that people would not like them, fears that their children would turn against them. Five were anxious about their health. Three had lost all ambition. Two felt they had no reason to live. Two were sometimes optimistic. And only one out of the 50 said she was truly happy.

Worry is a habit, and bad habits are broken only by substituting good ones. Day by day, work on new habits of positive thought. Begin now to think of all the blessings you have. Do not spend time wishing for things you do not have. Fear is a scarecrow that frightens away peace of mind. It is the enemy of a mature Christian personality. John writes, "There is no fear in love; perfect love drives out all fear" (1 John 4:18). And Peter says, "Humble yourselves, then, under God's mighty hand, so that he will lift you up in his own good time. Throw all your worries on him, for he cares for you" (1 Peter 5:6-7). The answer to worry and fear is trust in our Father who cares and can cope with our problems.

Many women allow themselves to be victimized by feelings of inadequacy. We as human beings are moral by nature. We not only act but also continually evaluate our behavior in terms of good and bad. Measuring ourselves by what we would like to be, we see how far short we fall of our ideal. Failure, sin and their accompanying guilt haunt us. We feel useless and worthless and deprecate ourselves. We should not confuse self-deprecation with humility. Humility is a Christian virtue. Self-deprecation is a self-centered vice. The self-deprecating woman says, "I'd teach if I could do it well. I don't know what to say to the sick. I'd visit, but nobody asked me." The woman with true humility says, "I'll try." She knows that her activity is for God and that he has promised to help. As Paul says, "The Spirit that God has given us does not make us timid; instead his Spirit fills us with power and love and self control" (2 Timothy 1:7).

How Do You Feel About Others?

Only when we have a proper understanding of God's love for us and of our own worth can we turn to others with a loving spirit. In reality, we are channels for the love of God which first flows into our hearts and then flows out to bless all whose lives touch ours.

What does your attitude toward others show about you? You will show a positive personality or a negative

16

one, an aggressive personality or a retiring one, a magnetic personality or a repellent one, depending upon how you relate to others. Christ in the heart is the key to interpersonal relations. The woman who has Christ in her heart will put each word and action to the four-way test that has been popularized by Rotary Clubs:

1. Is it true?
2. Is it fair to all?
3. Will it promote friendships?
4. Will it help all concerned?

Regulating our actions by this test will help us to follow Paul's admonition to "do good to everyone" (Galatians 6:10).

How Do You Meet Problems?

There are many ways we can respond to our problems. We can run away and disregard our responsibility. We can take enough aspirin to make us lose consciousness. Or we can stop and consider, decide and then do what is best.

To run away is easy. We revert to infancy and think, "If I don't see it, it isn't there." The ostrich does that. We can run away, but the problem stays. Many people make long trips and take expensive vacations to "get away from it all," only to find that their problems go along with them—inside them.

We can also escape into unconsciousness. You've read of how people consume millions of pounds of sleeping pills every year, not to alleviate pain but to put themselves to sleep. We hope that while we sleep the problem will solve itself or be solved by someone else. Alcohol and dope are also used for escape. As such deadening of the sensibilities becomes a habit, more pills or drinks are required.

Or we can face up to our problems and ask God for help. This alone can solve our problems. God's promises are sure, because he is "able to do so much more than we can ever ask for or even think of" (Ephesians 3:20).

Look Again

In the sixth chapter of Ephesians (verses 10-18), Paul has given us a picture of how the Christian should look:

He should wear a belt of truth. The major cause of mental illness is evasion, fear of the truth. Honesty and integrity help hold the personality together.

His shoes should be the Good News of peace. His attitude would be one of compassion, understanding, charity and love.

He should carry the shield of faith, a faith based upon study and prayer. He wears the helmet of salvation for protection. And his hands are busy meeting friends and foes with God's Word.

We should wear this wardrobe with prayer and supplication as we look often in the mirror to be sure we have our garments on straight.

QUESTIONS AND SUGGESTIONS

1. How can we examine ourselves in the light of scriptural teaching—really take a self-inventory of our strengths and weaknesses—without running the risk of becoming too involved with ourselves and becoming self-centered?
2. Can a person really be a Christian and be obsessed by worries and fears? (See Matthew 6:24-34.)
3. What is the difference between a humble person and a self-deprecating person? Think of incidents from Christ's life that indicate that his humility was a strong rather than a weak characteristic.
4. Make a list of the attributes of Christian character to be found in the Scriptures for study. Post the list in a conspicuous place and go over it often, examining your life and growth in light of these attributes.

Love Others

Scriptures for study:
Matthew 5:38-48
Romans 12:9-21, 13:8-10
Romans 15:1-6
I Corinthians 13
I John 3:11-18

Finishing Off the Devil

Helen Keller once said, "It is wonderful how much time good people spend fighting the devil. If they would only expend the same amount of energy loving their fellow men, the devil would die in his own tracks of ennui."

We certainly should give more thought to how we can love others. Love is the only way to face our troubled world; it is our only means of controlling the resentments that tempt us to sin; it is the only thing that gives depth

19

and meaning to our work; and it is the only way we can possibly follow Christ.

Facing a Troubled World

For so long, our world has been laboring under anxiety and deep apprehension, but has it not been so always? Each generation has, for one cause or another, suffered from fear of the future. Let us resolve to substitute compassion for this depression of soul concerning the world's miseries—compassion for those who have died and those who will die by violence, for the many children who are hungry, for the old who are lonely and helpless, and for the sick and suffering the whole world around. Compassion has a healing quality, for it is love with prayer, and God hears our prayers.

A famous philosopher once said of compassion: "If you feel this you have a motive for existence, a guide in action, a reason for courage, an imperative reason for intellectual honesty. Although you may not find happiness, you will never know the deep despair of those whose lives are aimless and void of purpose, for there is always something that you can do to diminish the awful sum of human misery."

There are five negative qualities which we can show in our dealings with others: fear, worry, doubt, impatience and anger, and nine ever-enduring positive ones: activity, compassion, friendliness, love, courage, generosity, tolerance, justice and cheerfulness. These enduring qualities must be our answer to our troubled world. They will express themselves through service to others. For Paul said, "Let love make you serve one another. For the whole Law is summed up in one commandment: 'Love your neighbor as yourself.' But if you act like animals, hurting and harming each other, then watch out, or you will completely destroy one another" (Galatians 5:13-15).

Controlling Resentment

In every group of people working toward some goal, there is at least one who is against everything and everybody. God put him there to give all the rest of the group a chance to practice tolerance and patience, kindness and understanding and love.

Resentments take hold and grow within us by refueling old fires. They cannot remain or grow if we "let go" and refuse to think about them. The truly humble person is one who has learned to refuse to refuel resentment. Blowing out the other fellow's candle won't make yours any brighter. In fact, it will put yours out. As John expressed it, "He who says he is in the light and hates his brother is in the darkness still" (1 John 2:9, RSV).

Ennobling Our Work

Work is love made visible. All work is empty unless there is love, and when you work with love, you bind yourself to yourself and to one another and to God. As Paul wrote to the Thessalonians, "There is no need to write you about love for your fellow believers. For you yourselves have been taught by God how you should love one another. And you have behaved in this way toward all the brothers in all Macedonia. So we beg you, brothers, to do even more. Make it your aim to live a quiet life, to mind your own business, and to earn your own living, just as we told you before. In this way you will win the respect of those who are not believers, and will not have to depend on anyone for what you need" (1 Thessalonians 4:9-12).

Imitating Christ

If Christ is first with us, we will give ourselves to other people, because he is the great giver. When we give, we receive, provided we have not given in order to receive. For Jesus said, "This is my commandment: love one another, just as I love you. The greatest love a man can have for his friends is to give his life for them" (John 15:12-13). "We love because God first loved us" (1 John 4:19). Let us resolve to respond to the love of God in the manner expressed in these lines:

> Because love has been lavished so upon me, Lord,
> A wealth I know that was not meant for me to hoard,
> I shall give love to those in need,
> Shall show that love by work and deed,
> Thus shall my thanks be thanks indeed, Dear Lord.

Creative Loving

True friendship is the first, necessary ingredient for proper relationships. It can be contrasted not only with hate but also with inordinate affection, which is love not ordered or kept within bounds—unregulated, unrestricted, immoderate and excessive. True Christian friendship is controlled and regulated by the love of Christ himself.

We all need one or two friends in whom we can confide and to whom we need give no explanation. Such friendship is centered not in each other but in Christ. Love includes more than friendship, but it must include real friendship.

Here are six basic rules for making and extending our circle of friends; in fact, for dealing with all people:

1. Value others. If you confer a benefit, never remember it; if you receive one, never forget it.
2. Sympathize, empathize. "Help carry one another's burdens" (Galatians 6:2).
3. Be sensitive to the emotions of others. "Rejoice with those who rejoice, weep with those who weep" (Romans 12:15).
4. Build trust. Be patient. True love comes slowly, but it is worth the wait. "Love is patient and kind....Love never gives up: its faith, hope and patience never fail" (1 Corinthians 13:4, 7).

22

5. Give of your time. Paul praised the Macedonians for giving themselves as well as their money to God's service (2 Corinthians 8:5). Dorothy Canfield Fisher once divided a woman's life this way: 20 years for herself, 20 years for her family, and 20 years for others. Today's woman will have an average life span of 76+ years, so her years for others should be increased to 25 or even more. There is no greater gift than a gift of time, which is a gift of oneself. But time is so precious and there are so many demands upon us that we must program our service to others. We will not find time; we must make or take time. If it is important to you to serve others, you will schedule time for this purpose. You will thus be following your master's example who "did not come to be served, but to serve" (Matthew 20:28).

6. "Let love rule your life." Read and practice 1 Corinthians 13. And remember: "Love ever gives, forgives, outlives, and ever stands with open hands. For this is love's prerogative while it lives: to give and give and give."

QUESTIONS AND SUGGESTIONS

1. What should be our attitudes toward those who wrong us, those who ask for things, our enemies, our brothers, needy brothers, strangers, those who persecute us, our fellow men, our neighbors, and the weak? Reread the Scriptures for study and list concrete things we can do to show love for these people.

2. Why does Paul tell us that it is important that we earn our own living? What other reason is evident from the Scriptures for study?

3. What can we do to bring ourselves closer to Christ and more into harmony with his example of perfect

love? Is it ever possible for us to attain to such a goal through efforts of our own?

4. Read 1 Corinthians 13 in every available translation. Type these on cards to remind you of the practical aspects of this great hymn to love. Memorize verses 4-7.

Lesson III

Love Yourself

Scriptures for study:
Mark 12:28-31
Luke 15:4-24
Romans 8:31-39
2 Corinthians 3:18
1 John 3:1-3

Reasons for Rejoicing

Each of ten young people was asked to name one thing in his or her character or personality which needed to be eliminated or improved. With little hesitation, they began to report their habits of procrastination, envy, impatience, withdrawal in social situations, lack of self-confidence, quick temper or sharp tongue.

Each of them was then asked to name one thing in his personality of which he was proud, one quality in which he rejoiced. They immediately became quite flustered and rather apologetic. It took time and prodding to get them to think of their good qualities.

This experiment has been repeated with a number of groups with much the same reaction. People are conscious of their limitations. They live with their failures and sins, but seldom consider their strengths and their virtues.

Even the boisterous and rude braggart or show-off, the one who appears to be an egotist of the first order, is often found on closer acquaintance to be a person who feels quite as inferior as the shy person who withdraws into his corner. This phenomenon is so common that it leads one to believe that there are no egotists in this world, only people who appear to be.

Two Basic Needs

Students of human nature believe self-acceptance or a feeling of one's own worth to be one of the basic psychological or spiritual needs of every human being. Another basic need is the need to belong to others, to be wanted and loved. These two needs seem to be inseparably linked in the life of each individual. Man, conscious of himself and others, must feel accepted both by them and by himself to enjoy life. One is quite as important as the other.

There is no escape from oneself. One can ignore God and refrain from speaking to fellow men. But who can escape from himself without withdrawing from reality and becoming a schizophrenic?

Jesus Is the Answer

Jesus, with his profound insight into human nature, indicates that he understands the worth of every human being in the sight of God and also the need for men to feel one another's worth and their own as well. He had a wonderful way of drawing publicans and sinners to him. They were searching for their own worth and redemption from guilt and rejection, and Christ knew how to help them recover their self-respect. Many heard him say, and doubtless believed his words, "Go your way and do not sin again," or "Your sins are forgiven; your faith has made you whole."

A Prerequisite to Christian Living

Self-acceptance is not only a joy in itself and prerequisite to the spiritual health of the individual, but it is also a prerequisite to living other gospel principles. A person, for example, who hates himself is not free to love his neighbor. He is afraid to give of himself and will likely use his neighbor and his faults to build up his own ego. And since he feels that he cannot elevate himself, he is likely to seek to bring his neighbor down to his own level through criticism and gossip. Starved egos are inclined to feed on others as parasites or cling to them as leeches. They do this quite innocently and unconsciously.

If one cannot accept himself, he is self-involved. This precludes the maturity of meekness and the open, inquisitive, teachable attitude of humility. A person who is so concerned with himself has great difficulty being objective, concentrating on his studies, pursuing a knowledge of the reality about him.

Similarly and tragically, the person without self-love often feels estranged from God. How can he be beloved of God, he reasons, when he hates himself? And even though it can be explained to him that God's love is constant, impartial and unmerited, this he cannot feel.

In the Savior's memorable summary of the Law, he spoke of two commandments, one like the other—love of God and love of neighbor. He also recognized a third person to love when he repeated the Mosaic admonition, "love your neighbor as yourself." Just what his thinking

27

was toward love of self, he did not, to our knowledge, explain. However, he obviously either took it for granted or affirmed it when he told us to love one another as ourselves.

The Christian woman loves herself—not in self-centered pride but in a true appreciation of herself as God's child and as precious to him. Christ placed such value on every person by his death to bring each salvation that we can no longer say "I'm not important," "It doesn't matter about me," "I'm a nobody." You are a precious soul, a person deeply loved by God.

Building Feelings of Worth

How then, we may ask, can a person build his feelings of worth on solid foundations? How can we, as Christian workers, and mothers, help others to find their own worth so that they will not destroy themselves in vain attempts to act important? The following are suggestions of needs which must be fulfilled before a person can know his own worth:

1. Man needs love. He needs to be accepted just as he is—not for what he can become or for what he ought to be—but for what he is now. "But God has shown us how much he loves us; it was while we were still sinners that Christ died for us" (Romans 5:8). We should follow our Lord's example in this as in everything and love each person we meet for what he is as we try to bring him to Christ.
2. Man needs success born of his own achievement. We all need desperately to excel in something. Although Paul warned, "Do not think of yourselves more highly than you should" (Romans 12:3), he did not say not to think of ourselves. We should think of ourselves with gratitude and thankfulness and use our abilities and talents with eagerness.
3. Man needs to repent. "Let us rid ourselves, then, of

everything that gets in the way, and the sin which holds on to us so tightly..." (Hebrews 12:1). Nothing destroys a person's feeling of worth as much as a sense of guilt born of sin. We cannot live without doing things that are wrong and that we recognize as being evil. Awareness of this gap between our behavior and our ideals destroys self-respect and estranges us from ourselves. We must accept the sacrifice of Christ, who "is able, now and always, to save those who come to God through him" (Hebrews 7:25).

4. We need to recognize the divinity that is in us. "Surely you know that Christ Jesus is in you?" (2 Corinthians 13:5). God breathed into us his breath. Our father is a King. Christ loved us so much that he died for us and rose from the grave and represents us. One soul is worth more than all the material world. He is preparing a place for us. Here is dignity, poise and power—all ours because of God's love.

Man is more than an animal and constantly to compare him to the animal world is to overlook his divine nature. He must be engaged in distinctly human endeavors. He has a mind which craves use and satisfaction. His capacity for emotional life is great. He needs to love and be loved. Man is an idealist; his eyes look to the stars. He is a dreamer; he beholds the moon. He has a memory, imagination and the power of reason. He who would know his own worth must live a distinctly human life—he must think, serve, imagine, belong, create, laugh and weep.

QUESTIONS AND SUGGESTIONS

1. What is the difference between the self-acceptance discussed in this lesson and the arrogant pride condemned in the Scriptures?
2. Discuss some of the personal blessings of

29

Christianity in which the Christian can take just pride. What other aspects of Christianity and the Christian's situation help to keep this pride in check?

3. Reread the Scriptures for study and discuss how each gives dignity and worth to the individual Christian.

4. Sit down and make a list of the five things you can do best. Beside each item on this list, think of a specific, concrete way you can use this skill or ability to God's glory and in helping others. Then do it.

Live Expectantly

Scriptures for study:
John 10:10
Romans 6:1-14, 8:1-17
1 Thessalonians 5:16-18
1 Peter 3:8-13

Christianity Is Life

Christianity is not just a theology. It is not possible to be a Christian without believing the right theology—that God is our Father and that Jesus Christ is his Son—but that is not all there is to Christianity. Christianity is not just a doctrine. It is essential that we accept the doctrine set forth in the Bible, but again, that is not all. Christianity is not merely a feeling, although the feeling or emotion of having accepted Christ will bring joy and strength to our lives. It is not just a profession. Our lives would be a constant profession of God's love for us and our responsive love for him. True theology, doctrine, feeling and profession are all parts of Christianity, but even their total does not make up the whole. Christianity is life.

Christ said that he came to give life—an abundant life. Let us as Christian women seek creatively to attain to this abundant life that our Savior came to give.

Find Life's Center

All too often, women "spread themselves too thin." We are all involved in the whirlwind of activities that present themselves to women today; it is easy to be like Martha and neglect "the good part." The Christian woman must locate life's center, define life's purpose and make the choices of daily life in view of that purpose. Each of us has a rule for living whether we are conscious of it or not. The following seems to be a safe rule of philosophy for the Christian to put into action: "Anything that dims my vision of Christ or takes away my taste for Bible reading or cramps my prayer life or makes Christian work difficult is wrong for me."

Live One Day at a Time

Christ taught us to pray, "Give us this day our daily bread." We don't need to burden ourselves by dragging along yesterday's problems or by reaching forward to catch hold of the worries of tomorrow. "There is no need to add to the troubles each day brings" (Matthew 6:34). Or, as the poet put it:

Three days I ween make up our life when sunshine and shadows play:
The day that is past and the day to come and the one that is called today.
But two are not ours at all, you see, for yesterday is

past and gone and tomorrow is in God's hands. Only today is given to us. Let us live it as best we can. This present moment is all we truly have. If we are to be happy, now is the time. If we are to be loving, now is the time. If we are to be of service, to share Christ with others, today is the day. Today is the tomorrow we were planning on with such bright hopes for accomplishment yesterday. "Today is the day to be saved" (2 Corinthians 6:2).

Live Trustingly

We must learn to accept God's plan for us with humility and with faith in his promises. We may not always understand, but we must always trust, realizing that he has given us life and is lending us material things while we are here. In his Word we learn that we leave all material and earthly things when he calls, for we brought nothing into this world and we take nothing with us (1 Timothy 6:7).

One practical bit of advice is to spend less money than you make. This can go a long way toward relieving our worries and anxieties. Paul recognized this truth when he said, "Be in debt to no one—the only debt you should have is to love one another" (Romans 13:8).

The story is told of Howard Christy that he tried to worry 15 minutes each day. Then he took time to fill up on God's Word. Each day he checked two passages in his Bible: "I can do all things through Christ who strengthens me," and "If God is for us who can be against us?" Soon Christy was not able to concentrate 15 minutes on worrying. If we do the same, and really believe God's promises, we will find worrying very difficult.

Live Prayerfully

Our faith and trust in God impels communication. Thus prayer comes as an expression of gratitude, a sharing of our emotions of love and appreciation, and a recognition of union with God.

Prayer is a force, not a form. It was Alfred Lord Tennyson who said,

> "More things are wrought by prayer
> Than this world dreams of. Wherefore, let thy voice
> Rise like a fountain for me night and day.
> For what are men better than sheep or goats
> That nourish a blind life within the brain,
> If, knowing God, they lift not hands of prayer
> Both for themselves and those who call them friend?
> For so the whole round earth is every way
> Bound by gold chains around the feet of God."

We should ask in faith, with patience and assurance. When we come to believe in prayer and to realize its power, it will become a constant part of our life and we will learn truly to "pray at all times" (1 Thessalonians 5:17).

God loves us as we love our children. There is nothing that concerns us with which he is not concerned, no matter how trivial it may be. He wants us to ask, to knock, to seek—any time, no matter where we are. He is listening.

Enjoy Beauty

Remember that God made the world beautiful—towering mountains, clear running streams, skies of beautiful colors, trees and grass and flowers. Take time to enjoy nature, to explore, to drink in its beauties. Jesus never seemed rushed. He took time to go out alone and pray. If we are too rushed to enjoy flowers, clouds and the rainbow, we are too busy.

We can see God in nature. "The heavens are telling the glory of God; and the firmament proclaims his handiwork" (Psalm 19:1, RSV). We can see God in the oak tree which was in the acorn, in the lily which was in the dry brown bulb, in the perfect laws that govern nature. They show God's care and guidance in our own lives.

Expect the Good

Finally, with our lives simplified and focused on God, we would live each day in positive relation to those around us. Here are some rules for expectant living:

1. Wake with expectancy. Don't look for trouble. Thank God first of all.
2. Don't take yourself too seriously. Look cheerful. Smile.
3. Say pleasant things. Forget unpleasantnesses.
4. Direct your thoughts. Think of the blessings of life. "Fill your minds with those things that are good and deserve praise: things that are true, noble, right, pure, lovely and honorable" (Philippians 4:8).
5. Control your emotions. Tell yourself, "I'm going to like people."
6. Believe in yourself, in others and in God.
7. Have a goal and work toward it, trusting God for the outcome.

John A. Schindler in his book *How To Live 365 Days a Year* advocated this set of rules for living: "Keep life simple. Avoid watching for a knock in your motor. Learn to like work. Have a good hobby. Learn to be satisfied. Like people. Say cheerful, pleasant things. Turn the defeat of adversity into victory. Meet your problems with decision. Make the present moment a success. Always be planning something."

Live expectantly!

QUESTIONS AND SUGGESTIONS

1. Among the Scriptures for study, John 10:10 and Romans 6:1-14 and 8:1-17 contain a number of words signifying the contrast between the Christian and the man of the world. Find these words of contrast and discuss their significance in the life of the Christian.

2. The passage which tells us to ask, knock, and seek is a part of one of the greatest lessons ever presented on Christian living. Who presented the lesson, what is it commonly called and where in the Bible is it recorded?

3. How can the Christian woman reconcile the Biblical emphasis on living one day at a time with her responsibilities to help her husband provide for their family? Can it be that we are putting more faith in guaranteed savings, social security and life insurance than in God?

4. As an exercise in finding your life's center, draw two groups of concentric circles like two bullseyes. In the first, define life's center as you think it should be. For instance, write "God" in the center circle, your husband's name in the second, your children in the third, and so on in whatever order you think your loyalties should lie. Then estimate the number of hours each week you spend on the various activities that take the most of your time. The roughest of estimates will do. Enter these activities in the second group of circles, beginning in the middle with the thing you spend the most time at. Compare the two circles to find the true center of your life and, if your circles don't match, pray to God to help you redefine your goals.

Lesson V

Follow Jesus

Scriptures for study:
Mark 8:34-38
John 14:1-7
1 Corinthians 10:31-11:1
Philippians 2:5-11
1 Peter 2:21-25

Pointing the Way

We travelled by car a great deal before there were road signs and when service stations were far apart. In those early days a stop for water, oil and gas, and to change a tire, was made at each station from Oklahoma City to Los Angeles. We would ask for information on conditions of the roads to the next town, and when we were ready to continue our journey, I always humiliated the others by saying, "Please point. We might start out in the wrong direction." When the station attendant said, "Four blocks that way," his raised arm and pointing finger assured us, and we confidently rolled on. He answered our question. He did not give a command. He pointed the way.

In three gospels, there is a record of four men who asked the Way of the Master. His directions were plain and pointed. Each man understood, as do all who are interested in the answer. These were not commands given arbitrarily. They were directions to a set destination.

Christ's Directions

Matthew tells us of the rich young ruler who asked, "What good thing must I do to receive eternal life?" (Matthew 19:16).

A lawyer who was a Pharisee (Matthew 22:36) asked, "Teacher, which is the greatest commandment in the law?" (Some scholars feel that the Scribe in Mark is also referred to as a lawyer in Matthew.)

The Scribe who had listened to Christ's reasoning wanted to know, "Which commandment is the most important of all?" (Mark 12:28).

Luke (10:25) tells us of a lawyer who stood up and said, "Teacher, what must I do to receive eternal life?"

Christ's answer to each of these is "love the Lord with all your heart and with all your soul and with all your strength and with all your mind and your neighbor as yourself." The brevity and beauty of this great commandment has never been equaled. Comprehended in its entirety, it includes the realization that, if a Christian is converted physically, mentally and spiritually, he will be eager to obey Christ and become a transformed person in thought, word and action.

God created woman with a heart for loving, a mind for learning and hands for giving, and woman should, in return, desire to grow in the ability to use these attributes in God's service. Christ's great commandment encompasses all. The Christian woman responds to this commandment by saying, "All that I am, all that I have, all that I hope to be, I dedicate to you."

Physical Sacrifice

Paul in Romans 12 challenges us, "Offer yourselves as a living sacrifice to God, dedicated to his service and pleasing to him. This is the true worship that you should offer (Romans 12:1). Socrates said, "Know yourself." Marcus Aurelius said, "Control yourself." But Christ says, "Deny yourself, take up your cross and follow me." He has led the way in sacrificial love, and we should try to follow his example. To realize that my body is the temple of the Holy Spirit, that it belongs to God, gives me a solemn sense of stewardship. I will seek to care for it properly and use it to his glory.

Mental Conversion

Paul continues by telling the church in Rome: "Do not conform outwardly to the standards of this world, but let God transform you inwardly by a complete change of your mind. Then you will be able to know the will of God—what is good and is pleasing to him and is perfect" (Romans 12:2).

A Hebrew philosophy holds that for everything there was first the thought, and for every thought there must be a thinker. First comes the thinker, designer and planner; then the thought, design or plan; and finally the revelation, the creation. The thing materializes as a result of the thought of the thinker, the plan of the planner.

In our areas of thinking, we seldom go beyond the thing to the thinker. We consider and often worship things and fail to go beyond them and bow in wonder and awe at the wisdom and greatness of the creator God.

When our minds have been changed, when we comprehend the greatness of God, understand his perfect laws in the earth and in the heavens which he created, and meditate on the laws he gave to his last creation, man, there comes a reverential awe which impels faith and which demands worship. To paraphrase Mark Twain: "Faith sees the invisible, believes the incredible, and is rewarded by the impossible."

The Christian woman is to love God with her mind. She is not to be content with ignorance when by diligent study she can know. She is not to bury her mental talent in a napkin.

Spiritual Growth

The Spirit is the motivating part of us as distinguished from the body and mind. It is a part which makes us different from the animal. It is God-given and answers to God. Spiritual growth comes by the desire to be like the Master. Knowledge of him and his plan comes by a knowledge of the Scriptures and by meditation and by prayer.

Spiritual growth is indicated by what the Bible calls the fruit of the Spirit: love, joy, peace, patience, kindness, goodness, faithfulness, humility and self-control (Galatians 5:22). This fruit is contrasted with evil desires and actions that are called the works of the flesh or of human nature (Galatians 5:19). The word "work" as it is used here carries with it the idea of unnatural activity. In this list is every evil, every repulsive and hateful characteristic. The wages of these activities is death. But the fruit of the Spirit, results of spiritual growth, are more like the fruit of the apple tree, which is borne painlessly, naturally, and for the use and enjoyment of others.

Jesus: Our Guide and Way

For such natural, fruitful development to take place, the Spirit and God's Word must find the good soil of a

40

receptive heart. Then we must concentrate on Christ and his example and ask ourselves, "What would Jesus do?" For Christ is not only our guide, the one who points out the way we should take, he is the way, the truth and the life, and we can never reach our destination of union with God except through him.

QUESTIONS AND SUGGESTIONS
1. What aspects of following Christ are brought out in each of the Scriptures for study?
2. Discuss the three areas of Christian conversion. Think of Scriptures that give guidelines for development in each of the areas.
3. Discuss specific, practical suggestions for achieving the transformation from self-directed to Christ-directed lives. Is it really possible for one to do this on his own?
4. Pick out one or two of the attributes called the fruit of the Spirit and study them in depth from the Scriptures. Looking up the words in a concordance is a good way to begin. Then organize your findings into a report that can be shared with others. If your schedule allows, one report on each of the attributes might be read at your next class meeting.

Grow Old with Christ

Scriptures for study:
Matthew 6:19-21
2 Corinthians 4:16-5:5
1 Timothy 5:9-10
Titus 2:1-5
Hebrews 5:13-6:3
1 Peter 1:22-25

Investments for Old Age

You will be old, unless you die young! There can be no more controversy about this statement. Its truth has been proven since God made man, and yet youth does not believe it. Young people will say, "My parents, poor things, can no longer care for themselves. What can I do with them?" But they don't realize that in a few short years their children will ask the same question.

"Prepare for old age. Get ready for this time when you are no longer active." This is an excellent admonition, but as is true with much advice, it is easy to give and hard to take. The donor of this suggestion, being young, is wise, but not until he reaches the stage in life when geriatrics has a meaning and he realizes that soon he will be retired will he realize how true were these words.

It is possible to make an investment in the noontide of life which pays sure dividends in old age. The cash for this guaranteed income can be paid over a period of years, and with each payment comes a pleasant deduction in your income tax.

Security for Children

I know a family who made such an investment. There were seven children and little else. But when the church doors opened, the family was there. Missionaries and visiting preachers were cared for in this home; the children were shifted out of their rooms and beds were made on the floor, but I don't remember any complaint. The father worked and the mother taught school after the seventh child was old enough to go to kindergarten.

This family lived within commuting distance of three excellent state schools, yet they kept Christian education always in mind. Over and over they repeated to their children, "You will go to a Christian college, you know." Finally all seven came through high school with good grades and were sent to Christian colleges. The mother and father sacrificed, and the boys and girls worked for part of their expenses. Little did they realize that the pattern of their lives was being formed there.

Four of them married Christians whom they met on the campuses, and the influence of the Christian college is evident in each family group. The oil royalties, the farm, the houses that were sold when, through the years, funds were needed to keep the boy or girl in school—these were not sold but were merely invested in character and Christian personality. Paul said, "Parents should provide for their children" (2 Corinthians 12:14), and "raise them with Christian discipline and instruction" (Ephesians 6:4).

Such an investment brings the greatest possible return and grows in dividends as the years turn brown hair to grey and then to white. How many elderly Christians do you know who are physically comfortable because of monetary investments wisely made in their prime but who are disconsolate and miserable because "the children and grandchildren have no interest in the Lord"?

Joy for Yourself

Other investments can be made in the form of those attitudes and ways of looking at life which can make growing old more joyful. First, you must be honest with yourself. Stop lying to yourself, passing the buck and rationalizing. You must face the truth of your aging; you must analyze yourself and work to overcome your faults.

Second, you must murder your worries in self-defense. Even giant trees fall because of small beetles. We all have worries, but we must learn to deal with them and seek their solution. Dig out your fears; exposure will kill them. The story is told of a lady who was having trouble sleeping, so she tried counting sheep. When she got to 50,000, she sheared them, made cloth from the wool, and made overcoats from the cloth. Then she lay in bed and worried about where she'd get the linings. There will always be something you can worry about, but the habits of prayer and trust can replace the habit of worry.

Third, bless yourself with the light touch. Develop a good sense of humor. Wrinkles in the heart extend to the face. An investment in joy is an investment in God's kingdom. For the kingdom of God is "righteousness and peace and joy that the Holy Spirit gives" (Romans 14:17).

The Christian woman has something to be happy about because she has been redeemed by Christ and knows salvation in Him.

Peace of Mind

Maturity should be marked by peace of mind. Peace of mind is not the absence of trouble, problems or worries; it is knowing how to handle them. It is gained through reliance on Christ, an investment which should be made early to pay the greatest dividends. For Jesus said "The world will make you suffer. But be brave! I have defeated the world!" (John 16:33).

A mature person is one who does not think only in abstractions but who is objective even when deeply stirred emotionally. He is one who has learned that there is both good and bad in all people and who walks humbly and deals charitably with all. He knows that, in this world, no one is all-knowing, and therefore all of us need love and charity, Christ and forgiveness. Peace of mind comes from accepting what cannot be changed. As Reinhold Niebuhr said, "O God, give us serenity to accept what cannot be changed, courage to change what should be changed, and wisdom to distinguish the one from the other."

Activity

As an investment in our old age, we should all make it a point to learn one new thing every day. We should take a greater interest in people. Age may bring physical weakness, but one can be mentally young at 80 if he puts his added experience, judgment and reason to good use in God's service.

The mature person has learned to recognize and use his ability and strengths. He is unselfish; he thinks of others. He is unafraid because his faith assures the ultimate outcome of his life. He chooses lasting values and is active serving God and his neighbors. Happiness is the result of activity in God's way. Make this your prayer:

"Let me do my work each day, and if the darkened hours of despair overcome me, may I still remember the bright hours that found me walking over the silent hills of my childhood, when a light glowed within me, and I promised God to have courage amid the changing years. May I not forget that poverty and riches are of the spirit. Forbid that I should judge others lest I condemn myself. Teach me to be thankful for life and for time's old memories that are good and sweet, and may the evening twilight find me gentle still."

Rules for Old Age

1. Believe and live your life in Christ.
2. Remember that you were young once. Have patience.
3. Don't bore people with your memories. Laugh at yourself.
4. People have to look at you. Make it easy.
5. Refuse to be slighted.
6. Don't bewail old age. Would you rather be old or dead?
7. Remember that morals don't change but customs do.
8. Don't discuss your symptoms. Everybody has them.
9. Be self-sufficient as long as possible.
10. Be cheerful. It takes only four muscles to smile, while it takes 14 to frown.
11. Keep your word. Be on time. Don't make people wait for you.
12. You've known since your birth that death is sure. There are great joys when we return to God. Be ready. Read your Bible and talk to your heavenly Father about all your affairs.

QUESTIONS AND SUGGESTIONS

1. Reread the Scriptures for study discussing the use of words dealing with the fleeting nature of the physical as opposed to the eternal nature of the spiritual.

2. Discuss the qualities possessed by a woman who has grown in Christian graces through a long life. Try to bring in points from the Scriptures for study as well as from your personal acquaintances with godly Christian women.

3. Contrast the joy that the Holy Spirit gives with the superficial "fun" that contemporary pleasure-seekers often find.

4. Begin now to try to learn something new every day. Start a list of interesting bits of information you pick up from books, television, people you meet. Begin to ask questions and develop an interest in more things. An inquisitive, open mind may be your investment in the future if you begin working toward it now.

The Christian Home

Scriptures for study:
Proverbs 12:4, 31:10-31;
1 Corinthians 7:1-5, 11:11-12
Ephesians 5:22-33
Hebrews 13:2-6
1 Peter 3:1-7

The Center of Life

Mental health therapists tell us that the following qualities are essential to a wholesome personality: 1) a feeling of security, 2) a sense of being appreciated, and 3) love and faith. It was these needs that first brought people together at the dawn of civilization. The family group gathered around an open fire to find safety, comfort and companionship. And these needs are still best met in the family situation, in the home.

A Christian home is no mere residence of the body. It is the place where affections develop, where children love and learn, where two people toil together to make life a blessing, and where the love of God can grow. It is the home which forms the character of each family member. Character is the result of the way we live and its effect on those around us. Current business and political standards are opposed to Christian character. In today's world, the philosophy is, "Nothing is certain except change." But Christian character traits never change, and the Christian home must remain constant. The stable home in a changing world is like a clear stream on a mountain—clean, wholesome, refreshing and life-giving. The home must be a place of activities which are conducive to strong Christian character. The home can be a center of criticism, bias and phobias, or it can be a place of love, tolerance and trust.

A home can conserve the good of previous days and stimulate a generation to create a better tomorrow. The life of the world can never rise to a higher level than that of the home. What we want the world to become must be what we make of the home.

A Home Must Be Built

A woman can buy a house, but she must build a home. A house is a piece of property located in a certain spot. We see many beautiful houses. A home, on the other hand, is a spiritual structure. It is wherever the father, mother and children are. Because it is spiritual, it cannot be seen. It must be felt and experienced.

Henry Ware once said, "A home is not an accidental or natural coming together of human souls under the same roof in certain definite relationships. It is a work of art to be builded upon fixed principles of life and action."

One of the saddest words in the English language is the word "homeless." The well-to-do are often homeless.

They may spend much time in hotels, cars and planes seeking change and excitement and trying to get away from themselves. The poor, too, are often homeless. Moving from place to place seeking employment, the poor may lose the sense of security and comfort that a home is to provide. However, moving doesn't have to destroy the home or defeat its purpose.

The story is told of a little girl whose family moved often during the World War II years. She once was heard to say, "We don't have a house, but we have a nice home." Obviously her parents had worked at building something stable in their lives of change.

Blueprint for a Christian Home

The following suggestions may help in the day-to-day task of home-building:

1. Learn to bear and forbear with one another. "Be humble, gentle and patient always. Show your love by being helpful to one another" (Ephesians 4:2).
2. Work together, play together and grow up together. ". . . We must grow up in every way to Christ, who is the head" (Ephesians 4:15).
3. Avoid the little quarrels; the big ones will take care of themselves. "So then, we must all aim at those things that bring peace and that help strengthen one another" (Romans 14:19).
4. Compromise (give and take). It is the anti-toxin of divorce. "Agree with one another, and live in peace" (2 Corinthians 13:11).
5. Practice sympathy, good humor and mutual understanding. ". . . The wisdom from above is . . . peaceful, gentle and friendly; it is full of compassion and produces a harvest of good deeds" (James 3:17).
6. Don't grouch before breakfast—or after it. "Love is not . . . irritable" (1 Corinthians 13:5).

7. Respect "in-laws." Don't criticize them and don't let their criticism come between you and your mate. "Accept one another, then, for the glory of God as Christ has accepted you" (Romans 15:7).
8. Establish your own house, even if it is just a one-room flat. "Make it your aim to live a quiet life, to mind your own business and earn your own living.... In this way you ... will not have to depend on anyone for what you need" (I Thessalonians 4:11-12).
9. Fight for each other but not with each other. "Get rid of all bitterness, passion and anger. No more shouting or insults! No more hateful feelings of any sort! Instead, be kind and tender-hearted to one another and forgive one another, as God has forgiven you" (Ephesians 4:31-32).
10. Build your home on religious faith and forgiveness. "Since you have accepted Christ Jesus as Lord, live in union with him. Keep your roots deep in him, build your lives on him, and become ever stronger in your faith" (Colossians 2:6-7).

Structural Weaknesses

Judge Mildred Lillie gives the following as major causes of trouble in the home for which women are responsible: nagging, carelessness about personal appearance, lack of interest in the home, carelessness about money, lack of encouragement to the family.

A woman's love, cares and duties are constant; they never change. The qualities exhibited by the worthy woman of Proverbs are still the best answer to the causes of divorce listed by Judge Lillie.

The proverb teaches us that a worthy woman is a good investment. She is industrious and energetic, and she knows how to do a job, so she is able to direct others in their work. Such a woman is not the type to use money unwisely. "The heart of her husband trusts in her, and he will have no lack of gain."

The worthy woman knows her pantry and is able to prepare meals. She decorates her house with good carpets and tapestries. She cannot be faulted for lack of interest in her home.

She is not careless about her appearance but makes herself clothing of "fine linen and purple" in addition to providing warm and attractive clothing for her family.

"She opens her mouth with wisdom; and the teaching of kindness is on her tongue." She certainly doesn't nag.

And she encourages her husband and children. This we can surmise from the good reputation her family enjoys and from their lavish praise of her.

A Woman's Place

The members of today's family are scattered in business, office and schools, and in these different environments, they develop separate interests which often make family conversation and communication sketchy and hurried. Home becomes a place where the members come to get ready to go.

For all this diversity, there remains this fact: patience and love can form a cohesion. This is the mother's job, and no other can accomplish it. Building a home requires time, planning and sacrifice. But woman's work in the home is not compelled labor when there is love for husband and children.

When a woman paints a great picture, writes a noteworthy book or makes a mark as a doctor or lawyer, much is made of it. A woman's achievements usually are made while her first interest is in loved ones and home. Woman's greatest masterpiece cannot be duplicated by man. She creates a well-ordered home, a secure and reasonably happy household, and an atmosphere of companionship which nourishes the human mind and spirit.

53

QUESTIONS AND SUGGESTIONS

1. In a day of hate and fear, of people living closer together physically but further apart in understanding and love than ever before, what specific activities might we plan in which we could open our homes and our hearts to those around us?
2. List the activities in which the worthy woman of Proverbs 31 was engaged. For what was she known?
3. What can we do to give a firm sense of continuity to our homes and make them a place of security in a changing world?
4. In seeking to build a better home, ask yourself the following question: What will my child remember about his home? When you can be reasonably satisfied with your answer, you can be sure that you are doing your best in building a Christian home.

God's Plan For Christian Motherhood

Scriptures for study:
Luke 2:40
Ephesians 6:1-4
Colossians 3:18-21
2 Timothy 1:5, 3:14-15

Mothers Make the Home

One of the loveliest homes I ever visited was in a three-room unpainted house in West Texas. It was made up of a mother who did not finish high school, a father and four boys. The mother could not buy bread, so she made it. Then she used the flour sacks to make curtains and tablecloths and, with print strips joining white sacks, pretty bedspreads. She always kept the floors and wood-work clean, and she was always happy at the end of the day to welcome her family home.

It was as we learn from Proverbs 15:17: "Better is a dinner of herbs, where love is, than a fatted ox and hatred with it." God's plan is plain, and every Christian mother, by study and prayer, will build into her life loyalty to her husband, home and family. The mother in large measure creates the atmosphere of the home.

Lessons from the Bible

Love cannot be commanded. It must be won by repeated tenderness and devotion. Children are told to honor their parents, but parents must live before them in such a way that this admonition is easy to carry out. Isaac was an honor to Sarah and Abraham. John the Baptist honored Elizabeth and Zacharias. We do not even know the name of Judas' mother, but how we pity her. Once Judas was a beautiful baby and she loved him, but he certainly did not bring honor to her.

We can learn from the examples of other women of the Bible. From Ruth, we learn loyalty and the ability to say, "Where you go, I will go." From Hannah, the mother of Samuel, we learn of prayer, patience, industry and sacrifice. And from Mary the mother of Christ, submission to God and faith in his plans.

Mary had the greatest honor a human mother could attain. She must have been the loveliest of all Jewish maidens, carefully reared in the faith of her fathers—a virgin selected by God to give birth to and to nourish through infancy and childhood the promised Messiah. She did not understand the immaculate conception, but she accepted this miracle of life and tenderly cared for God's Son all the way to the cross, where he bore her sins and ours.

Spiritual Training

Parents influence not only the physical and mental characteristics of their children through heredity, but also, by training, their attitudes, outlooks and future actions. The mother must not underestimate her importance. She is the most influential teacher her child will ever have. "Train up a child in the way he should go, and when he is old he will not depart from it" (Proverbs 22:6, RSV).

For example, the church needs missionaries. Parents can talk up this need, study geography and interest their children in helping take the gospel to other people.

Mothers select many of the family's friends and extend hospitality to those selected. This is one way to teach children—by the example of godly people that you invite into your home.

A sense of wonder and awe is characteristic of younger children. You can help develop it in the heart of your child. Walk with him into God's great outdoors so that he may see the flowers, the sunshine, the moonlight, the clouds, the raindrops, the wind-bent trees, the snowflakes. All of these which cause wonder and gratitude can also be the basis for the development of a sense of reverence and worship. God the great creator is greater than any of his creations. Let us lift up the hearts of our children to his majesty and love.

Study and Teach Children Early

You are daily Bible readers, and each day you should read to your children, and have them read to you as soon as they are able, from God's Word. God's plan is that mothers should be an example, should teach in every way. This means that you must lead your children in Bible study, in prayer, and in attending worship services.

Parents can do much to make going to church a

pleasure. Get ready on Saturday night, and get off on time. Get the roast partly cooked, and potatoes, carrots and onions ready to put in, the night before. If this isn't done, go anyway. If you and your children arrive at services frazzled and harried, none of you will be ready to worship God.

There should be a time to study for Bible class during the week. Two boys were overheard talking about their Bible class lessons. "Yes, I know all about Abraham, Isaac and Jacob," one of them said, "But we haven't come to Jesus yet." Parents must be alert to what their children are studying in Bible classes and be able to supplement this learning, remembering that we are not teaching unrelated stories or facts but building Christ-like character.

Mothers must be informed and able to talk to their husbands and children. Have a grasp of community, state, national and world events so you can communicate with your teenage children and discuss current affairs in relation to the changeless truths of the Bible. Answer as many of your children's questions as possible. If you don't, someone else will. Be a good listener.

Duties of Mothers

The responsibilities of mothers toward their children have never changed. The Christian mother must:

1. Prepare herself mentally, physically and spiritually for motherhood; study herself, study books and study God's Word. ". . . That your love will keep on growing more and more, together with true knowledge and perfect judgment, so that you will be able to choose what is best" (Philippians 1:9-10) .

2. Care for her children in three ways: mentally, physically and spiritually. "If someone does not take care . . . of his own family, he has denied the faith and is worse than an unbeliever" (I Timothy 5:8).

3. Love them as they are, even when they are naughty,

with no comparisons. "Love does not keep a record of wrongs" (1 Corinthians 13:5).

4. Teach them to make decisions, not always "because I say so" but "Let's consider all the angles."
5. Be emotionally balanced. "Be still, and know that I am God" (Psalm 46:10).
6. Guide by precept and example. Be consistent in discipline. Always tell the truth.
7. Help her children to make life's adjustments and yet to be decisive in holding to eternal principles. "Our purpose is to do what is right, not only in the sight of the Lord, but also in the sight of men" (2 Corinthians 8:21).
8. Love the Lord with all her mind, strength and might and her neighbor as herself.

Mother the Great Example

As a Christian mother you must be, first and foremost, a Christian. You must teach your children God's plan, prepare them to live with courage and to assume responsibility, encourage correct values of body and mind, and read the Bible and pray with them.

To do this effectively, you must constantly maintain good lines of communication with your children. Talk to them. Be interested in ballgames, school and fusses. They must be conscious at all times that you are for them, you believe in them, you treasure them, you are honest with them, you discipline them for their good and you love them.

Pray constantly that God will give you the strength and grace to send your children into the world on the path he has chosen for them.

QUESTIONS AND SUGGESTIONS

1. Using the Scriptures for study, discuss the duties of

parents toward their children as regards spiritual training.
2. How can parents fulfill the Biblical admonition to discipline their children (see Proverbs 13:24) without running the risk of discouraging their children or driving them away?
3. Much is said these days about hypocrisy. How can parents avoid the charge of hypocrisy while teaching and living Christian lessons before their children?
4. Study the Bible on the subjects of the home and family life and have a family group discussion on ways of improving your home life.

Christian Motherhood Today

Scriptures for study:
Luke 10:38-42
Philippians 1:9-11, 4:10-13
1 Timothy 2:9-15, 4:6-10, 5:13-14
Titus 2:4-5

Three Kinds of Women

Some time ago, Pearl Buck wrote an article on "America's Gunpowder Woman." She said that by nature American women fall into three groups. The first and smallest of these groups is that of the Talented Woman. These women are driven to do a special work day after day, mentally, physically and spiritually.

A second and larger group has an all-consuming vocation as well, but in this case, it is the home. This group is completely satisfied mentally and spiritually with the activities of motherhood and housekeeping. So long as the four walls stand, the Domestic Woman is contented, busy and useful. She is a comforting, essential creature who perfectly fulfills her being.

Both of these, the Talented Woman and the Domestic Woman, are safe and contented since they know what they want and are doing it.

The Gunpowder Woman

The third and largest group Miss Buck calls the Gunpowder Woman, and although she does not explain the name, I'm sure we can understand just what she means. The Gunpowder Woman is restless and may explode any minute.

There are millions of families who do not know actual want for necessities. The mother does not have to work to keep her family from starving; her children are adequately clothed; and her house is better than her forebears ever dreamed of. This mother has a normal interest in her husband and children, but after she cares for their needs and tidies up the house, she finds that she has surplus time, energy and ability which she does not know how to use.

And so she becomes one of thousands of women in offices, in stores and in industry who have no special interest in their work but are there because of restlessness. Though she does not intend it, before long the competition to keep her job means a tired wife and mother who, instead of being at home to greet the family, often is the last to reach home base.

The Value of a Mother

Miss Buck says that this mother may seem unselfish in her desire that her children have all that the Jones children have, but that she herself is worth more to them than all the toys, furniture and cars she might provide. Her children come home from school full of things to talk about, and there is no mother to listen. They are frustrated and emotionally hungry, and half of them develop serious mental and emotional problems.

The Christian woman who earns a salary is likely to overdo and go beyond her strength both emotionally and physically. An honest day's work for pay, and then she has to hurry home to make up to her husband and children for all her time away from them.

Does this gunpowder mother know her children? Where they are? Who their friends are? What they read and see on TV and in the movies? Is her salary actually needed? Does she consider values and make plans, or is she an immature person?

Today it is imperative for some families to have two pay checks to make ends meet. Sometimes it is best for the woman to work outside the home. But before such a decision is made, ask several questions:

What does my husband think of the plans? The Scriptures teach the headship of the man. A pay check is not worth family disruption.

What will its consequences be on my children? I must remember my stewardship of my children's souls as well as their bodies. Remember that household conveniences can wait but the brief 18 years of child training are soon gone. Especially the preschool years deserve a mother's constant care.

Will it add to or detract from our happiness and Christian mission as a family?

Christian Maturity

Christ demands mature commitment to our responsibilities. The Christian life includes enough opportunities for study, prayer, devotion and service to others to fill a number of lives, if we only consider what activities will have lasting value.

Dr. William Menninger, the well-known psychiatrist, says that most of us do not grow up, that we are infantile in our emotional life. He says that, if and when we realize this and begin to be mature persons, we will have solved the problem of our nation's shortage of hospital beds, for half of them are currently occupied by mental patients.

He lists five qualities which a mature person must have. These qualities are essential to the Christian mother today who wants to make proper value judgments:

1. Sincerity. If there were not deception, there would not be a sense of guilt. We must learn to seek one another's good with sincere and open hearts. "Love must be completely sincere" (Romans 12:9).

2. Personal integrity. We must learn to be honest with ourselves, to find our job and do it. When Boaz was aware of Ruth's interest in marriage, he was exceedingly careful to do the honorable and ethical thing. Naomi, his kinswoman, said, "He will not rest until he has settled the matter today" (Ruth 3:18, NEB) .

3. Humility. Humility means teachability. Only the humble can learn. Is there a wise and understanding man among you? He is to prove it by his good life, by his good deeds performed with humility and wisdom" (James 3:13). Humility is the proper attitude of the child of God before his all-wise heavenly Father.

4. Courtesy. Courtesy is more than just being polite. It is rising and offering your chair to an older person because you know that, if you were they, you would appreciate it. It is the Golden Rule in practice. It

includes hospitality, kindness, gratitude and appreciation. It is the wife whose husband said of her, "She treats me like company." "Love is not ill-mannered" (I Corinthians 13:5).

5. Wisdom or spiritual life. God's spiritual laws are as invariable as his natural laws. The law of gravity is no surer than the law that you will reap what you sow. How do we gain this wisdom? Through "the Holy Scriptures, which are able to give you the wisdom that leads to salvation through faith in Christ Jesus" (2 Timothy 3:15).

Instilling Mature Attitudes

The Christian mother must not only concentrate on her own maturity and mental health, but also instill healthy attitudes in her children. Mothers must teach Christ's forgiveness. He forgives, so we can forgive ourselves. Mothers must teach proper attitudes toward sin. Such teaching begins before the child can talk or walk, because children sense what we believe about right and wrong.

Mothers must encourage all efforts for social and civic good because of the influence social conditions might have on their children's welfare. We cannot do away with all the sin and evil in the world, but we must do what we can do to improve things. However, we must be careful not to get so involved with providing a good environment for our children that we neglect the children themselves.

Consider the thought in Helen Gorn Sutin's verse:

Busy, busy, busy, busy,
Meetings everywhere,
The rise in child delinquency
Has brought about a scare.
PTA and guidance groups
Are strictly on the ball

With welfare clubs and benefits,
And I respond to all.

Lectures, lunches, conferences,
Colored slides or tea.
I listen and confer like mad
On child psychology.
The welfare of our children is
A noble cause, and fine—
My only trouble seems to be
I have no time for mine!

QUESTIONS AND SUGGESTIONS

1. What worthwhile activities could a Gunpowder Woman be engaged in besides holding down a job if her income were not absolutely essential to her family's well-being? If the income must be supplemented, what productive work might she be able to do at home?
2. Making the choices of life requires a great deal of wisdom. What does the Bible teach about wisdom and how to receive it?
3. Discuss the qualities of a mature person listed by Dr. Menninger with reference to the woman who is trying to decide what is best to do with her time.
4. Make a schedule of the way you spend your time for several days during the week. Study these schedules prayerfully to determine if you are really making the best use of your time. List several specific, worthwhile ways you can spend any spare time you might have in service to others, in Bible study and prayer, or in growing closer to your husband and children.

The Christian Woman's Influence

Scriptures for study:
Matthew 5:13-16
1 Corinthians 5:9-11
2 Corinthians 2:14-17
Philippians 2:14-16
Colossians 4:5-6
1 Timothy 3:2, 7

Practicing Christianity

Mahatma Gandhi, statesman, philosopher and Hindu leader, was a Bible student. He made a pilgrimage to Rome with the determination of becoming a Christian. He had been converted to the doctrine of Christ and wanted to share in its peace and brotherhood. However, he returned to India a disappointed man, with the observation that Christianity is a beautiful religion, but that it is not practiced by those who profess it.

The earliest mark of a Christian was how he treated his fellow men. "See how they love one another," was said of the early church. This quality of love made them different from others, a peculiar people.

Such an active, working faith should characterize the church today. Christianity can never make an impact on the world until the world sees each of us acting like a Christian. The Christian woman, especially, has a great potential for leading others to Christ through her life and example.

A Woman's Sphere

Woman holds within her nature a potential power to influence or mark lives. This does not mean only the strong, masterly woman. It is just as true of the weak or weepy type. For good or ill she will mark most deeply those she loves the most. The power of a woman's influence cannot be over-emphasized.

They talk about a woman's sphere as though
it had a limit.
There's not a place in earth or heaven,
There's not a task to mankind given,
There's not a blessing or a woe,
There's not a whispered yes or no,
There's not a life or death or birth,
That has a feather's weight of worth
Without a woman in it.

Are you aware of the influence you have? Are you constantly, prayerfully seeking to use it for greater service to God? One national magazine has had the motto for years, "Never underestimate the power of a woman." Women live longer than men. They do most of the spending and selecting. Man builds the house, but woman makes the home. It is her spirit of love, understanding and service which creates its atmosphere. Her influence should shine brightest at home.

God made everything else before he made woman. He looked at Adam and saw that he was lonely, so he made woman to help man. She helps lighten his burdens. Her influence and responsibilities are great.

Christian Influence outside the Home

We glibly blame the home, and usually the mother, for all that is wrong with the world. Can she counterbalance the evils in the neighborhood? unteach the false learning of the schools? combat the effects of filth on TV and in movies? Can she offset the pressures that tempt teenagers to sin? The home no doubt is the greatest molding influence for good or evil, but a woman's concern must go beyond her four walls to a world in need.

The Bible teaches that we must keep ourselves unspotted from the world (James 1:27). Many seem to think this means that we should separate ourselves from the world and have as little to do with the issues and activities of our times as possible. But this is not the example that our Lord gave us. He went where the people were. He teaches us to resist evil, not hide from it. And he prayed to his Father and ours just before his death, "I do not ask you to take them out of the world, but I do ask you to keep them safe from the Evil One" (John 17:15).

The Christian woman can exercise a great influence for good in government and civic life. However, she must do so with great care and consideration. She must carefully consider the time it will take and set her priorities so that her commitment to home and family are not neglected.

There are myriad calls on a woman's time. Often the choice is not between the good and the bad but, as in the case of Mary and Martha, between the good and the better. Think carefully before you choose what outside activities will be given your attention. Here are some questions to ask:

1. Does this group stand for justice and right living?
2. Will I be helped to become a better mother or wife or person by belonging to this group?
3. Will this add to my usefulness in my home or in my service to God?
4. Have I the time to give without neglecting my first responsibilities?
5. Will I be happy in the group and can I contribute to its success?
6. What will it do for my influence for Christ?

If my time for Christian service is lessened, if Bible study is shortened, if prayer is interfered with—this group is not for me.

Christ Must Be First

There are countless women's organizations which will compete for your attention. Some of them such as the Parent Teacher Association offer opportunities for service and influence for the Christian woman. In making the choices of where best to use our influence, however, we must remember that Christ and his church must come first in our lives. The assembly of the saints must not be relegated to second or third place. I like the attitude of one woman who was very talented and in demand to participate in many civic and study groups and explained, "I never say 'no' to the church. Other activities must fit in after this allegiance." However, we must remember that we are to be the light of the world— not only the church— and to let our light radiate we must not cloister ourselves completely. On the other hand, let us be sure that we let our light shine in these groups and that our candle is not snuffed out by worldly temptations and influences.

When the gospel meeting is being advertised, call

your civic friends. Three fine women that I know were invited to morning services by a friend who was in an organization with them. They became interested in the church from this contact and now have Christian families. When we have coffees or teas for our Bible classes, we can invite two or three outside acquaintances to meet the Christian group. Let us never forget that our purpose in life is to glorify God whether in the home, church or outside organization.

As a member of an organization, the Christian woman can be an example of Christian service by diligence, faithfulness, joy and unselfish love. However, if you join a group and then show yourself to be unreliable in carrying out your responsibilities to it, your membership may do Christ's cause more harm than good. For Paul told the Colossians, "Whatever your task, work heartily, as serving the Lord and not men" (Colossians 3:23, RSV).

In other words, membership in civic, service and social groups gives us an opportunity to let our lights shine to God's glory before people who might otherwise not come in contact with Christian people, but we must guard ourselves to practice what we profess. Most people we contact will judge us by the criteria expressed by Edgar A. Guest in the following poem:

> The lectures you deliver may be very wise
> and true
> But I'd rather get my lesson by observing
> what you do
> For I may misunderstand you and the high
> advice you give,
> But there is no misunderstanding how you
> act and how you live.

QUESTIONS AND SUGGESTIONS

1. Discuss those aspects of Christian character which are most likely to make the greatest impact on

those about us. How can we develop these aspects of character?

2. Read Matthew 6:1-18. How can we reconcile this with our responsibilities as lights of the world?

3. What are some of the organizations and opportunities for service that Christian women might be able to support in your area? Discuss ways of making the influence of Christian women better utilized in your area.

4. Think of your individual opportunities for contacting other people. If you don't have any opportunities but have time, try to get some. Then use these opportunities to God's glory by carrying out your duties in a Christian way, by praying for guidance in approaching your associates with God's Word and by doing all in your power, with wisdom and with love, to win them for Christ.

Woman's Work in the Church

Scriptures for study:
Romans 12:3-8, 16:1-6
Ephesians 4:1-6
Philippians 4:2-3
James 2:14-26

What Is the Church?

The church is the family of God. As a family, it is a permanent association —time and distance do not affect its union nor the love which exists between its members. A family lives in a house, and so does a church. But, just as with the family, the church is not a house; it is people! Family ties are not dissolved when the children leave the house, and in a similar way, we are in the church wherever we may be. We cannot be in the church on Sunday and out on Monday.

The church of Christ is made up of followers of Christ—those individuals who believe in him as the Son of God and trust him as their Saviour. As a demonstration and confirmation of this faith, they confess his name, are buried in baptism with him for the remission of their sins and rise to walk a new life. The Lord adds the saved to his church. This is how the church has been formed since its beginning on the day of Pentecost (Acts 2).

God gave us the church for many reasons, one of which was the same reason that he gave Eve to Adam, that we might enjoy companionship. Through the church, we are able to share our burdens, strengthen one another, praise God the Father and magnify Christ the Son. We have fellowship, partnership and love as children of a common father. If you love God, you will love the church.

By the same token, if you love God, you will be careful to live uprightly before those outside the church. Just as children can bring honor or dishonor to their families, so our conduct reflects on our family, the church.

Our Work in the Church

Woman's work in the church begins when she is born into God's family and is concluded on earth when she leaves to join the family in Heaven. Because she loves God, she is sensitive to the service which she can perform, and because it is her responsibility to do what she can, she does not wait to be asked. Because of this love, she is impelled to serve God—impelled, not compelled by command.

Years ago, Herman Wilson sent a questionnaire to a number of preachers, educators, elders and editors. It went something like this: 1) What do you consider to be the chief problem in the Church today? 2) What tendencies are most dangerous? 3) What are your suggestions for improving the work of the local congregation and the church at large?

The answers were varied, but they showed remarkable agreement. Lack of spirituality just about sums them up. Lack of spirituality means that one does not know Christ. One may know about him and be able to quote most of the Bible and yet not know the Christ about whom it is written. Believing is a command, but it cannot be forced. It is a response to one who said "When I am lifted up from the earth, I will draw all men to me" (John 12:32). It comes from knowing how God loves us and how Christ our Saviour took our place on the cross. It is trusting him for salvation and strength for Christian living. When we really begin to understand his atonement and abiding presence, we as Christian women will be much more eager to do the Lord's work and will be able to do it much more effectively as we appropriate the power which he has promised.

Areas of Service

God needs women to serve in his kingdom today! He needs women who love the poor as did Dorcas (Acts 9:39) and who are willing to spend hours assisting them, sitting up with them when they are sick, ministering to their needs. God needs women like Eunice and Lois (2 Timothy 1:5) who will teach their children and the children of others the Word of God from infancy so that the children may have a deep and abiding faith in God's Word and be willing to dedicate their lives to it as did Timothy.

God needs women like Priscilla (Acts 18:26) to do personal work. There are women in every neighborhood who need to be taught the Word of the Lord more perfectly. He needs women who will place the hearing of God's Word before cooking and housework or purely social affairs, as did Mary (Luke 10:39) when she sat at Jesus' feet. God needs hospitable women like Martha

75

(Luke 10:38) and the Shunemite woman (2 Kings 4:8). There is so much to be done, and women can do so much.

A. R. Holton used to say that woman power was the greatest untapped resource in the church. Give us Christian women and the church will grow. The men will be influenced for the better. The gospel will be spread. The good name of the church will be upheld.

More than 50 percent of the members of the church are women. Often they are the best workers and the most devout. Often they have more time for volunteer service than the men. Because women are not to preach or to be the elders does not mean that there is not a great task for them to perform, as they did in Bible times.

Women are stewards of their talents. They are to be faithful in the use of their talents, not being content to criticize what others do nor to refuse to do what they can do because it does not seem to be as impressive as the work of others, but humbly to serve. God rewards according to faithfulness.

This adaptation of a poem by Rudyard Kipling points out that despite the differences in our abilities, there is important work for each of us to do in the church:

The church is like a garden that is full of
stately views,
Of borders, beds and shrubberies and lawns
and avenues.
With statues on the terraces and peacocks
strutting by;
But the Glory of the Garden lies in more than
meets the eye.

For where the old thick laurels grow along the
thin red wall,
You find the tool and potting sheds which are
the heart of all.
The cold frames and the hot house, the dung

pits and the tanks,
The rollers, carts and drain pipes, with the
barrows and the planks.

And there you'll see the gardeners, the men
and prentice boys
Told off to do as they are bid and do it without
noise;
For except when seeds are planted and we
shout to scare the birds
The Glory of the Garden it abideth not in
words.

And some can plant begonias and some can
bud a rose
And some are hardly fit to trust with anything
that grows;
But they can roll and trim the lawns and sift
the sand and loam
For the Glory and the Garden accepteth all
who come.

The church is like a garden and such gardens
are not made
By singing:—"Oh, how beautiful!" and sitting
in the shade,
While better men than we go out and start
their working lives
At grubbing weeds from gravel paths with
broken dinner-knives.

There's not a pair of legs so thin nor yet a head
so thick,
There's not a hand so weak and white nor yet
a heart so sick
But it can find some needful job that's crying
to be done

For the Glory of the Garden glorifieth
everyone.

Then seek your job with thankfulness and
work till further orders
If it's only netting strawberries or killing slugs
on borders;
And when your back stops aching and your
hands begin to harden,
You will find yourself a partner in the Glory of
the Garden.

Oh, Adam was a gardener, and God who
made him sees
That half a proper gardener's work is done
upon his knees.
So when your work is finished, you can wash
your hands and pray
For the Glory of the Garden, that it may not
pass away!
And the Glory of the Garden it shall never pass
away!

QUESTIONS AND SUGGESTIONS

1. Study all the Bible references that define the church and discuss the implications of the various words used to describe it: family, body, house, etc.
2. What can we, as individual Christian women, do to increase our spirituality?
3. Discuss areas of service open to women in your congregation. Include in your discussion both the specific programs of the church and the individual opportunities that are available to each of you in your community.

4. Christ taught about people with various talents and their responsibilities to use these talents, no matter how many or how few they might have. In order to do this, list your talents—abilities, time, money—that might be used in God's service. Then plan to use at least one each week for the next few weeks in the service of your fellow man and to the glory of God.

LESSON XII

The Christian Teacher

Scriptures for study:
Colossians 3:l6
1 Thessalonians 5:l4-15
2 Timothy 2:l4-26
Titus 2:3-5
1 John 4:13-16

Every Christian a Teacher

Every Christian woman teaches every day. She teaches by the words she says. She teaches by what she does. She teaches by the decisions she makes as she meets life's challenges. She teaches by what she fails to say. Whether or not you ever participate in a Bible class program, in a personal work effort or even in telling your friends about Jesus, you will teach people by your example.

However, the true Christian is to do more than teach by her life. She is to teach, as did her Lord, in "word and deed." We should teach because we have been commanded to teach, because it is our individual responsibility, because we must teach to follow Christ's example and the example of the early church and because we will gain so much from our teaching.

Teaching Is Commanded

After the resurrection, Christ met the disciples on a hill in Galilee. "When they saw him they worshiped him, even though some of them doubted. Jesus drew near and said to them: 'I have been given all authority in heaven and on earth. Go then, to all peoples everywhere and make them my disciples'" (Matthew 28:17-19). These were among our Lord's last words.

Christians are told to "have reverence for Christ in your hearts, and make him your Lord. Be ready at all times to answer anyone who asks you to explain the hope you have in you" (I Peter 3:15). And God said to Ezekiel, "If I say to the wicked, 'You shall surely die'; and you give him no warning, nor speak to warn the wicked from his wicked way, in order to save his life, that wicked man shall die in his iniquity; but his blood I will require at your hand. But if you warn the wicked, and he does not turn from his wickedness, or from his wicked way, he shall die in his iniquity; but you will have saved your life" (Ezekiel 3:18-19, RSV).

It Is an Individual Matter

We have an individual responsibility to teach. Every Christian must teach others. Just as baptism and partaking of the Lord's Supper are individual and no one can do them for us, so is teaching by individual Christians necessary in order for them to be scriptural followers of Christ.

Twenty-two scriptures show the necessity of taking the Lord's Supper, 120 scriptures teach on the subject of baptism, but 1,000 times in the New Testament we are exhorted to teach the Word.

Each Christian woman must teach. She should feel impelled to tell of Christ. The nature of the gospel requires it. Good news must be carried by individuals to individuals. The mass is reached only as the individuals composing it are reached.

Jesus said, "Teach all nations," "every creature." He did not say, "Invite them to come," but "Go teach." Not "Let them know you are in town," but "Go teach." Not "Come" but "Go."

You might be thinking that this is all good and well— for men. But what about us as women? Remember Christ's sermon to the Samaritan woman? As a result of his teaching, she taught and brought "great multitudes." But it is not necessary to have such a large audience. Priscilla and Aquila taught Apollos, and see how the effects of their teaching spread!

Christ and Early Christians

Christ is our example as the ideal teacher. He used every opportunity to teach people about God.

The early church taught. "And every day in the Temple and in people's homes they continued to teach and preach the Good News about Jesus the Messiah" (Acts 5:42). After Stephen's death, the church was scattered, but "The believers who were scattered went everywhere, preaching the message" (Acts 8:4).

You Will Gain

Perhaps even more than the person you are teaching, you will gain from the experience of offering God's Word to others. First, you will gain the clear conscience and happy feeling that comes from doing what you can to help other people. Doing good is a satisfying experience to all of us, but lingering doubts that we have done our best can make us miserable.

Second, you will learn from the study you do to prepare to teach. When you feel that you must understand something well enough to communicate it to someone else and to be able to answer any questions they might have about it, you will do your very best to master the material. Thus you will find that your study in preparing lessons for others will be among the most worthwhile study you will do. Also, the lesson will be reinforced in your mind as you first, prepare the lesson; second, present the lesson; and third, explain again any points that may not have been understood.

Third, you will gain as one always gains from having done God's will and from following the example of Christ. We grow spiritually as we come closer into communion with Christ and into harmony with God's will for us.

How Should We Teach?

Christians may teach on an individual basis, in a group or class situation, by distributing gospel literature and by preaching from the pulpit or through mass media. They may teach by lecture, discussion, question or conversation. They may teach in the classroom, in the home, on the street, on the job— anywhere there are people. Your teaching methods and procedures will depend on your individual talents. But the important thing is to teach.

The way a thing is presented has as much to do with its being accepted as what is presented. Teaching should be the result of love guided by wisdom. Christian women in their teaching should be "wise as serpents and harmless as doves." Never emphasize your opinion; but read and emphasize God's Word. Never enter into heated controversy; but point to God's Word. Be sure the love shines through in all your teaching. Remember you are not seeking to win an argument but to win for Christ an immortal soul.

Aims of the Teacher

The teacher must try:
1. To help her pupils know God.
2. To teach them to follow Jesus as leader and accept him as Savior.
3. To help them come to know the Bible.
4. To teach God's plan for life as well as his plan of salvation.
5. To develop Christian character.
6. To help her pupils become working Christians.
7. To teach them to share in building Christian homes.
8. To lead them in translating Christ's teaching into Christian service.

The church needs trained workers. The plumber knows how to use his tools; the doctor is trained in diagnosis and treatment; the teacher must be prepared and trained in using her tools. You should have your own Bible, keep it with you, and use it. Be familiar with it, and mark it so you can find passages easily.

Teachers should be mature Christians. The person who has been a Christian 10 years, and by study and prayer has grown in spirit, may be more mature than she who was baptized 40 years ago and has in the meantime neither been nourished by the Word nor strengthened by prayer. It may be as the Bible says that "There has been enough time for you to be teachers—yet you still need someone to teach you the first lessons of God's message" (Hebrews 5:12).

The teacher must know the facts about God and his plan, and these she comes to know by studying his Word. She must also know God. We know God through Jesus Christ by putting our learning to the test, by living according to his pattern and by a life of prayer and communion with him. And this is eternal life: for men to know you, the only true God, and to know Jesus Christ, whom you sent" (John 17:3). This is life's great quest.

QUESTIONS AND SUGGESTIONS

1. Using the scriptures for study, discuss who, what and how the Christian woman should teach.
2. We are commanded to teach. However, just how effective do you think the teacher would be who teaches solely "of necessity"? Could the principle of 2 Corinthians 9:7 be applied to our giving of our time and talents in teaching?
3. Have we discharged our responsibility to teach when we invite others to worship services? Is it essential that we do the teaching ourselves, or might we be able to invite our neighbors into our homes for Bible study and then ask someone else to lead the discussion or present a lesson?
4. How can you grow in knowledge of God and in knowledge of his plan? List several specific ways and try to put them into practice so you will be able to teach others more effectively.

The Church Leader's Wife

Scriptures for study:
Philippians 1:9-11
1 Timothy 3:1-13
Titus 1:5-9
James 5:14-18
1 Peter 5:1-4

Not All Are Leaders

We may not all be wives of elders, deacons, preachers and teachers, but just as all men should develop those traits of character which outfit them to assume responsibilities in the church, women should work toward developing those traits which would make them suitable helpers for Christian leaders.

Duties as a Christian

The first duty of the church leader's wife, as is true of any Christian, is to know God. The church leader's wife must be a devoted Christian. She must be at peace with herself. This does not mean that she should be self-satisfied, but rather that she must always do her best and work to improve herself without becoming discouraged. Her trust in Christ and her recognition of his grace and his constant presence with her will give her "God's peace, which is far beyond human understanding" (Philippians 4:7).

The church leader's wife must be cooperative, be able to give and take, and be willing to assume duties. She should seek to give credit to others and be willing to accept blame. She will be helped by believing the proverb "It is amazing what you can accomplish if you don't care who gets the credit."

She must look for the best. There are two kinds of people in the world— those who see a cup as being half full and those who see it as being half empty. The church leader's wife should belong to the first group. She should seek and expect to find good from people and situations. The Christian is essentially an optimistic realist. If you love people and look for their good points, you will be amazed at how much good you will find. Seek to be the kind of friend who is not seeking to have her friend after a visit say, "Isn't she wonderful?" but instead, "Isn't God wonderful?" and "I like myself better after I have been with her."

The church leader's wife must be hospitable and thoughtful. She must develop empathy as well as sympathy. She should not be critical and should learn to give others the benefit of the doubt. "Do not judge others, so that God will not judge you" (Matthew 7:1).

In sum, the church leader's wife should desire to develop her talents fully, help others freely and serve God faithfully.

Duties as a Wife

God's first plan for woman was that she be a companion and helper to her husband. The church leader's wife will have special responsibilities because of her husband's duties, but basically she must be the kind of wife that all of us should try to be. She will love her husband above all others. She will be one with whom he can share confidences and discuss problems. Have you noticed how much the Bible speaks of bridling the tongue?

She will encourage her husband and have faith in his abilities. She may make suggestions, but she should always be constructive in her criticism. She should make her suggestions at the right time and in private.

She will pray for and with her husband.

She will not request or require too much of his time or attention. Many a selfish wife has hindered her husband in his leadership role because she demanded that he perform so many small chores at home. Many a wife has hindered her husband because she resented the time he spent in church business meetings or resented his financial liberality to the church. She should encourage him in every good work by going with him or cheerfully sending him to visit the sick, sad and lonely.

Duties as a Mother

The church leader's wife will be a busy woman, but she should never allow herself to neglect her duties to her children. These duties, and the power to shape lives that is a mother's, have been pointed out by E. C. Baird in these words:

There is a kingdom called the home
Where mother reigns as queen.
The treasures fair that cluster there
Not elsewhere may be seen.

She loves this kingdom of the home,
And there she builds her throne;
The things of earth that bless the earth
Find here a safety zone.

Here children live in blessedness,
Protected by her love;
With gentle sway she leads the way
Through wisdom from above.

Her word, her smile, her soft caress—
She rules her realm with these;
With humble heart she does her part,
And conquers on her knees.

Other Duties

New Testament writers describe the mature Christian wife as being chaste, meek, quiet, reverent, a teacher of that which is good, kind, full of good works, a keeper at home and a laborer in the gospel.

The church leader's wife should be an example of these attributes to her children and to other Christian women. She should seek to excel in her roles as wife, mother, neighbor, teacher, visitor, church worker, comforter and counselor.

Preparation for Service

The Christian woman who aspires to this role should prepare for her service through regular study of God's Word and through a program of reading good religious books and periodicals as well as through prayer.

A list of suggested books would include *Gift from the Sea* by Ann Morrow Lindberg, *God's Woman* by C. R. Nichol, *Women of the Bible* by Edith Deen, *Christian Home* by P. D. Wilmeth, *You Can Be Beautiful* by Lottie Beth Hobbs, *Woman to Woman* by Eugenia Price, *Time Management for Christian Women* by Helen Young and Billie Silvey and *Fitting It All Together* by Peggy Collins and Linda Olivet.

Women might also subscribe to such religious periodicals as *21st Century Christian, Power for Today* and *Christian Woman* Magazine, and in addition to brotherhood news publication such as the *Christian Chronicle* or *Gospel Advocate.*

God's Word, of course, will be the center of her reading and the yardstick by which she gauges the truth and helpfulness of other publications. John Greenleaf Whittier wrote,

We search the world for truth.
We cull the pure, the good, the beautiful
From graven stone and written scroll—
From old flower fields of the soul!
Weary seekers of the best,
We come home laden from the quest
To find that all the sages said
Is in the Book our mothers read.

But study is not enough. The church leader's wife must have learned to apply what she reads to her daily life. "To look is one thing," said Macdonald McNair. "To see what you look at is another. To understand what you see is third, to learn from what you understand is still something else. But to act on what you learn is all that really matters. "So then, everyone who hears these words of mine and *obeys* them will be like a wise man who built his house on the rock" (Matthew 7:24).

The church leader's wife must grow through learning, living, serving, giving, worshiping and winning others for the Lord. Such growth comes by *desiring* to grow, and by *believing* that, with God's help, spiritual growth can be realized.

Do not compare yourself with others, for all of us have varying talents, but compare yourself with your own faith and hope and love and knowledge of last year or the year before. Life is a growth process, and some of us are children, some adolescents and some more mature, but all of us are acceptable as we seek to grow in faithfulness. Most of all, let us compare ourselves with our perfect pattern for living, Jesus Christ.

QUESTIONS AND SUGGESTIONS

1. From the scriptures for study, discuss the qualifications of the church leader's wife, including in your discussion not only those things said specifically about the wife but also those things said about the church leader which indicate areas his wife might be able to help him in and duties she must be understanding of.

2. Discuss the difference between the wholesome optimism discussed in this lesson and the attitude which refuses to see realistically the evil that is in the world.

3. The church leader's wife, and indeed all of us, must grow in the ability to share. Especially must we learn not to be jealous of our husband's interest, time and attention. Read 1 Corinthians 7:32-34 and discuss it in the context of our first responsibilities.

4. Make it a point to read at least one religious periodical or book this week.